Toucan

Jessica Coupé

AV2

www.openlightbox.com

Step 1
Go to www.openlightbox.com

Step 2
Enter this unique code
XSLGCFWO1

Step 3
Explore your interactive eBook!

AV2 is optimized for use on any device

Your interactive eBook comes with...

Contents
Browse a live contents page to easily navigate through resources

Audio
Listen to sections of the book read aloud

Videos
Watch informative video clips

Weblinks
Gain additional information for research

Slideshows
View images and captions

Try This!
Complete activities and hands-on experiments

Key Words
Study vocabulary, and complete a matching word activity

Quizzes
Test your knowledge

Share
Share titles within your Learning Management System (LMS) or Library Circulation System

Citation
Create bibliographical references following the Chicago Manual of Style

This title is part of our AV2 digital subscription

1-Year Grades K–5 Subscription
ISBN 978-1-7911-3320-7

Access hundreds of AV2 titles with our digital subscription.
Sign up for a FREE trial at www.openlightbox.com/trial

Toucan

CONTENTS

Meet the Toucan

Toucans are among the most well-known birds in the world. These rainforest birds have round heads and big eyes. Toucans also typically have short wings and sturdy legs.

Most toucans have black feathers on their bodies. The feathers on their necks and throats are bright. A toucan's most unique feature is its large, colorful beak.

A Tropical Bird

Toucans are a group of Central and South American birds. They live in warm, wet forests, such as South America's Amazon Rainforest. There are about 35 **species** of toucans. Different species have unique feather and beak colors. Large toucans, such as the toco toucan, weigh about as much as a pineapple.

Social Birds

Toucans prefer to be with other toucans. They often live and travel in groups called flocks. A toucan flock can include more than 20 birds. Toucans are noisy birds. They use sounds to tell each other about food or danger. Toucan sounds include squawks and frog-like croaks. Toucans get their name from the sound of these croaks.

Toucans live in the top part of a rainforest. This area is known as the canopy.

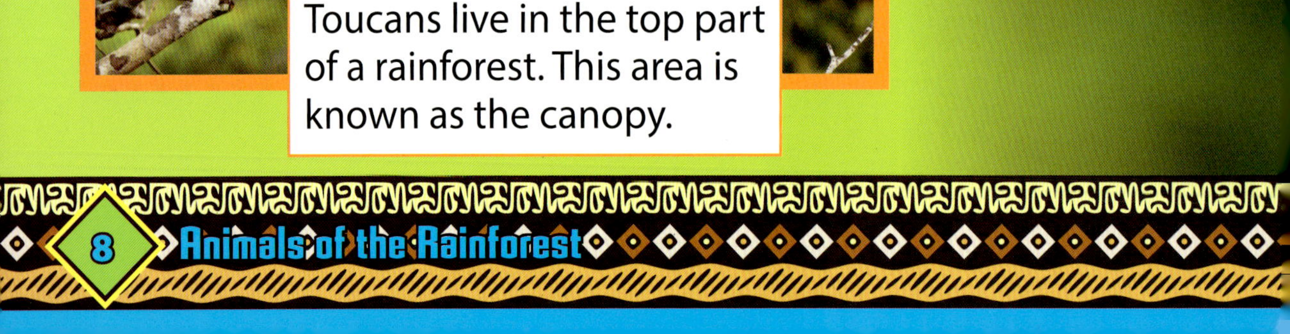

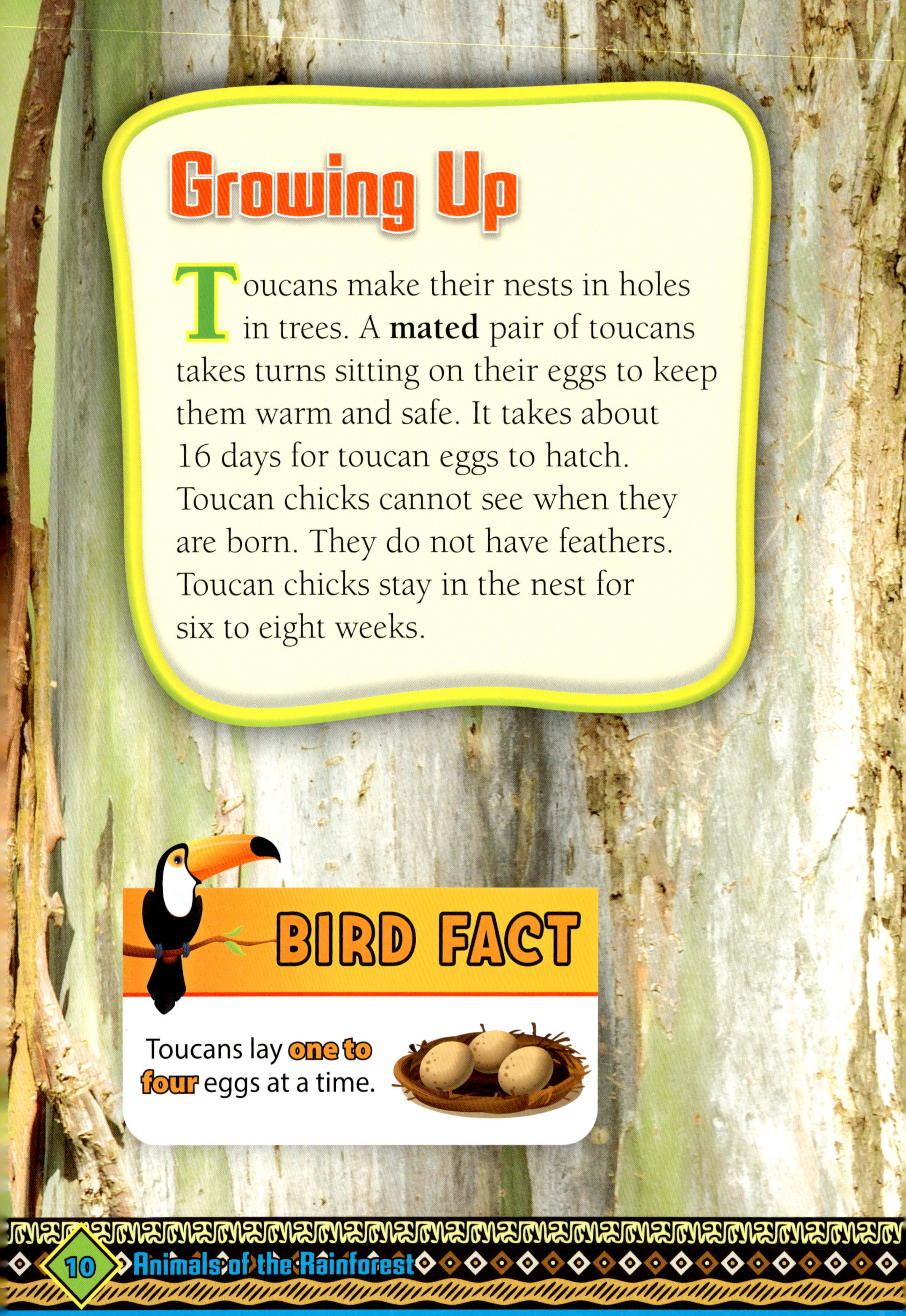

Growing Up

Toucans make their nests in holes in trees. A **mated** pair of toucans takes turns sitting on their eggs to keep them warm and safe. It takes about 16 days for toucan eggs to hatch. Toucan chicks cannot see when they are born. They do not have feathers. Toucan chicks stay in the nest for six to eight weeks.

BIRD FACT

Toucans lay **one to four** eggs at a time.

A Closer Look

Toucans have **adapted** to their **habitats**. They have unique features that help them survive in their environment.

Tongue

A toucan has a long, narrow tongue. Bristles on the side of the tongue help the bird grab and eat food.

Wings

A toucan has small wings. This makes it hard for the bird to fly. Instead, toucans often move by hopping between tree branches.

Eyes

A toucan has good eyesight. This helps the bird spot threats in dark forests.

Beak

Although large, a toucan's beak is very light in weight. The length of a toucan's beak allows the bird to grab distant food easily.

Feet

A toucan has two toes that point forward and two that point backwards. This helps it grab branches and climb around on trees more easily.

Blending In

The colors on a toucan's face, neck, and chest may include yellow, orange, white, and blue. They may help the birds blend in among the colorful leaves and fruits in the rainforest's canopy. Toucans also have colorful markings on their beaks. The bright colors of a toucan's beak may be used to help it attract a mate.

A toucan's colors may also help the bird recognize other members of its species.

Toucan

Big Beaks

A toucan's beak is about four times the size of its head. The outside of the beak is made from **keratin**, the same material that makes up human fingernails. The birds release heat through their beaks, which cools them off in hot weather. Toucan beaks have **serrated** edges. This helps the birds grab and tear objects.

BIRD FACT

Toucan beaks can be about **7.5 inches** (19.05 centimeters) long. This is about the length of a banana.

Toucan
17

A Wide Diet

Each day, toucans start searching for food early in the morning. They mostly eat fruit. A toucan eats by grabbing and tearing food with its beak. Then, it throws back its head to swallow the food with the help of its bristly tongue. Along with fruits, toucans will eat flowers, insects, frogs, lizards, and the eggs of other birds.

Toucans spread seeds when they eat fruit. This helps the plants that grow from these seeds to reach new places.

Toucan Conservation

Many toucan species are widespread across Central and South America, so most can be found in large numbers. However, some rainforests where toucans live are being cut down so people can build roads and homes. This can make it difficult for animals to find food. Toucans are also hunted as trophies or pets. These threats mean that some toucan species today are in danger of **extinction**.

Yellow-browed toucanets are an endangered toucan species. They are only found in a few places in Peru.

Amazon Rainforest Bird Conservation Status
EX
Extinct
EW
Extinct in the Wild
CR
Critically Endangered
EN
Endangered
VU
Vulnerable
NT
Near Threatened
LC
Least Concern
Banded Cotinga
Harpy Eagle
Toco Toucan

Toucan Quiz

1 How long can a toucan's beak be?

2 What do toucans mostly eat?

3 Which animal do some toucan calls sound like?

4 Where do toucans nest?

5 How many eggs do toucans lay at a time?

6 What is the outside of a toucan's beak made from?

7 Why does a toucan have bright colors on its face, neck, and chest?

8 On hot days, what does a toucan's beak help it do?

ANSWERS **1.** 7.5 inches (19.05 cm) **2.** Fruit **3.** Frogs **4.** Holes in trees **5.** One to four **6.** Keratin **7.** To blend in among the colorful leaves and fruits in the rainforest's canopy **8.** Lose heat and cool down

Key Words

adapted: changed to suit an environment

extinction: being no longer alive anywhere on Earth

habitats: places where animals live, grow, and raise their young

keratin: a hard substance that makes up animal body parts such as beaks, horns, and claws

mated: a pair of animals that have had young

serrated: having a jagged edge like a saw

species: a group of related living things that can reproduce

Index

Get the best of both worlds.

AV2 bridges the gap between print and digital.

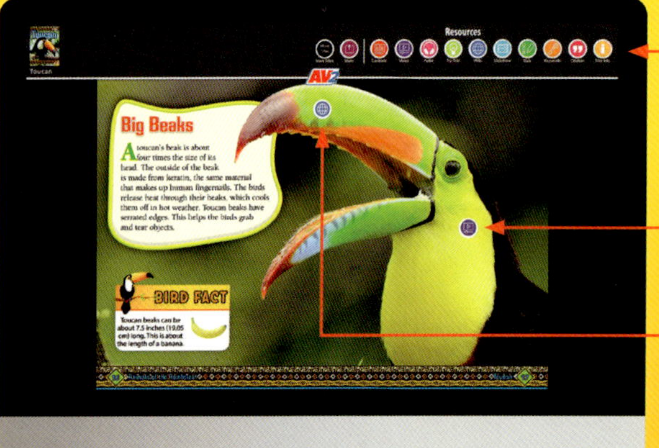

The expandable resources toolbar enables quick access to content including **videos**, **audio**, **activities**, **weblinks**, **slideshows**, **quizzes**, and **key words**.

Animated videos make static images come alive.

Resource icons on each page help readers to further **explore key concepts**.

Published by Lightbox Learning Inc.
276 5th Avenue, Suite 704 #917
New York, NY 10001
Website: www.openlightbox.com

Library of Congress Control Number: 2022934784

ISBN 978-1-7911-4775-4 (hardcover)
ISBN 978-1-7911-4776-1 (softcover)
ISBN 978-1-7911-4777-8 (multi-user eBook)

052022
101121

Printed in Guangzhou, China
1 2 3 4 5 6 7 8 9 0 26 25 24 23 22

Project Coordinator: John Willis
Art Director: Terry Paulhus

Every reasonable effort has been made to trace ownership and to obtain permission to reprint copyright material. The publisher would be pleased to have any errors or omissions brought to its attention so that they may be corrected in subsequent printings.

The publisher acknowledges Alamy, Getty Images, Minden Pictures, and Shutterstock as its primary image suppliers for this title.